ROMANCE OF A SOUL

(Facts About Yogi M.K. Spencer's Three Births)

ROMANCE OF A SOUL

Yogi M.K. Spencer

Aravali Books International (P) Ltd.
New Delhi-110020

1st Edition 1954
2nd Edition 1955
3rd Edition 1998
ISBN 81-86880-48-8

Romance of A Soul
Rs. 35/-

Publishers : Aravali Books International (P) Ltd.
W-30, Okhla Industrial Area, Phase-II,
New Delhi-110020
Phones : 6911417, 6841564
Fax : (011) (91) 6849782

Printed at : Aravali Printers & Publishers (P) Ltd.
New Delhi-110020

Rishi Ram Ram

DEDICATION

Dedicated to Fakir Shirdi Sai Baba in whose form God was seen by Yogi M.K. Spencer.

and

to Rishi Ram Ram, a great Master in the Spirit World who was the Guardian Spirit of Spencer's soul from his very birth throughout his life,

and

to the memory of the divine souls of Yogi M.K. Spencer and his spiritual comrades H.M. Spencer and K.S.D. Aiyer

and to

all earnest seekers of God realization today and tomorrow.

CONTENTS

ABOUT THE AUTHOR

Minocher K. Spencer was a Parsi Spiritual seeker, intellectual, medium, spiritual healer and a great Yogi who preferred to remain away from the hustle and bustle of social life. Right from his birth he was under the care and guidance of Rishi Ram Ram – a great Spirit Master in the Spirit World. He was keen to see God 'face to face' and was prepared to undergo all sacrifices. He engaged himself in meditation and writing spiritual books based on his vast study of Spiritualism and Comparative Religions and divine revelations and messages received by him from various Spirit Masters, Spirits and God Himself. God had assigned to him the mission of writing books to spread spiritual knowledge in the world. He wrote about a dozen valuable books.

The present book contains the unique autobiography of Yogi M.K. Spencer's soul which had taken only three human births on this earth plane and finally merged in Spiritual Plane in 1958. In the first birth in the 13th Century, this soul became an Italian Christian Monk, the famous Saint Petricio, the Founder of the 'Holy Order of Friars' whom the Christian world still remembers with great veneration. In second birth, the soul incarnated as a Hindu woman in South India, most probably in the 18th Century. In the third birth, the same soul incarnated as Minocher K. Spencer in a Parsi family in India. In this third birth, the soul's greatest yearning to realise God, see Him face to face, and have divine assurance not have any more rebirth, was surely fulfilled due to the unique love and rigorous spiritual training imparted by his Spirit Guide and Master Rishi Ram Ram and by God Himself whom Spencer venerated and envisioned as Fakir Sai Baba (Shirdi Sai Baba). How he was able to achieve God realization by the unique efforts of Rishi Ram Ram and God Sai Baba is vividly and most thrillingly described in Yogi Spencer's hitherto unpublished spiritual memoirs entitled *HOW I FOUND GOD* (1957).

Rishi Ram Ram and God in the form of Sai Baba Himself had revealed and dictated this great soul's autobiographical accounts of the three births.

Yogi M.K. Spencer was a metal merchant in Karachi. He was a very eager spiritual seeker.. He became a medium and he could commincate with the Spirits of the Spiritual planes. He was a spiritual healer. He was a dedicated social worker. Serving the lepers was his lifelong hobby. *Ahura Mazda* (Parsis call God as *Ahura Mazda*) in the form of Fakir Sai Baba (Shirdi Sai Baba) prepared him to become an Adept and His Missionary. God assigned to him the mission of writing great spiritual books, most important of which was 'HOW I FOUND GOD', and these he wrote with the help of innumerabe spirit messages received in mediation from the Master Spirits of Rishi Ram Ram, Christ, Buddha, Krishna, Raman Maharishi, Meher

Baba. Zoroastra etc. He was divinely inspired to compose many highly inspiring poems on God, Devotion, Soul and such spiritual themes. He was a most unique spiritual *Sadhka* with whom God Sai Baba did a number of spiritual feats like entering his soul, extracting his soul, allowing his soul to see the God's Plane and communicating with God, Spirit Masters and other souls etc.

Having known this background information about the great Indian Yogi M.K. Spencer, about whom most people in India and abroad still do not know, readers of this book will be able understand and appreciate the spiritual genius of this unique God's emmissary and Yogi of our times.

The main importance of this book '*Romance of a Soul*' for all people of the world lies in the fact that this book clearly reveals that inspite of a man having led a highly religious life and spreading one's faith with boundless dedication and devotion or serving others with great empathy and sympathy, the soul of that person is not liberated and has to take rebirth, because of the mistakes like condemning others' religions while eulogising one's own religion, or too much attachment with one's children or the like, Unless one's soul is purged of all attachments, ego problems and *dwandas* (dualities) and is fortunate enough to get a Guru to guide and help in self-realisation or God-realization, *mukti* from the cycle of birth and death is not possible. This thrilling story of Yogi Spencer's soul in all the three births should be an eye-opener to all *sadhakas,* religious *pracharaks,* saints, and all those householders who are eager to achieve *mukti* in their lives.

We express our gratitude to Yogi Spencer for having left behind such a priceless treasure of spiritual knowledge for the humanity to ponder over and learn the divine secrets and thus to be in a position to improve their lives morally and spiritually.

I am grateful to Sri A. Somasundramji, my Spiritual Father, and Spirit Master Swami Amritanandji for giving me this unique opportunity of editing this book and bringing it out under the auspices of the Sai Divine Research Centre, at Faridabad.

13 May, 1998 **Prof. S.P. Ruhela**

PREFACE

The manuscript of this book has been sent to the present writer with a request for a short preface. The request is accompanied by a special message saying:

> "Kindly tell Homi that it is Ahura Mazda's order, which he must obey, that he should write a small preface of not more than one or two pages, recording the authenticity of the messages and apprising the world of the fact of the book *How I Found God*".

In willing and respectful obedience to this command, the writer craves leave to point out that the person through whom the message was received has been known to him as one who has been daily, nay hourly, in touch with Ahura Mazda for a number of years now. The writer therefore has no hesitency in declaring that the messages which form the text of this book are not of human but spiritual origin. This is borne out completely by the very nature of their contents.

Though the identity of the soul, the romance of whole careers through its last three incarnations on earth is decribed in the following pages is not mentioned, it is not difficult for the reader to establish it. The reference to his book, *The Other World*, and to his other books on Spiritual Philosophy and Religion, published through THE SPIRITUAL HEALING CENTRE of Coimbatore, is enough to show who he is. His latest publication *How I Found God* and a perusal of this volume will convince any one how well the author has been trained by God for the Divine mission which is spoken of there and in the pages of this tract.

Romance is something, which as this book says, is "unusually colourful and picturesque in man's life," Can any thing be more colourful, more picturesque and more ennobling than the triumph of a soul in its fight against the forces of evil and in the assertion of the divinity of its own true inherent nature? If you wish to read of such a romantic triumph read this small book as an introduction and then read *How I Found God* for an accurate detailed account of such a triumph.

Homi S. Spencer

INTRODUCTION

Christ was born at Bethlehem in a Stable yard, without any comforts of life, unknown to any one, that in the infant newly born God had chosen His emissary for spreading a great Mission, a great Religion on the earth plane. God works His miracles in a wondrous way. All prophets, saints and seers, born in life, carry out God's orders and His plan as ordered by Him. Just as a seed sown in the garden takes root and gradually grows into a plant or a tree and gives fruit or flower and then decays gradually, every human soul born in life, evolves according to its nature and past experiences and eventually leaves the body which it occupies only temporarily to gain experience. Countless incarnations are required before the soul realizes its own perfection and its own divinity. When this consciousness is gained, the soul no longer seeks habitation in a human body. It becomes spirit by itself – the spark of God, without any separate identity.

This is the life's end *viz.*, to transform the soul into spirit, to disentangle the soul from the meshes in which it is entangled and covered and clear its way for perfect freedom in the universe. So long as the soul is entombed in human body, it is its bondage. It gains freedom only when it transcends all limitations and gains consciousness of its divine origin.

Man acts in life as if he were concerned with his body only. He first seeks to satisfy his bodily needs. He wants to cover his body, nourish it and keep it in comfortable condition. Bodily needs are necessary, for so long as soul dwell in the physical body, the latter has to be recognized as its Temple. But this temple of the soul has to be kept bright and shining. It shines the best when it is clothed the least; when it is nourished not with rich wines and choice dishes but with simple food of a few varieties only.

The body is not the reality. It is a temporary cover of the soul – the temple of the soul. Keep it clean and pure. If the body is polluted by excessive drink and food, or by the abuse of the senses, the indwelling soul becomes dejected. The doorway to its emancipation is clogged and barred. It gets more and more entangled in the web of its sheaths which act like iron clamps, fastening the soul to the body.

The soul which is a spark of God is the reality; not the body, not the senses, not the mind. Emancipation of the soul from the body is God-realization. It is to understand what God is, to understand the mysteries of the universe, to understand the truths of life, which lie deeper in human consciousness and which require to be exposed for human benefit.

God-realization is not a contact with any entity in its transcendental garb. It is realization of the fact that man is a spark of God – a spirit, endowed with all the faculties, deeply rooted in some transcendental depths, embarked upon a voyage, mysterious in its origin, but with this consciousness that its kinship is with God and its sole objective is to seek the good of others without a flaw in the perfection of his character, without a spot on the escutcheon of his conduct, without a speck on the white sheet of his aura. This is self-realization. This is God-realization.

When a man attains this stage, his soul becomes free. It can then leave the body when it likes. It can travel in all parts of the universe. It occupies the body not as a prisoner clamped down to its donjon but as a chariot driver, leading the body, the senses and the mind, as it likes. A liberated soul is the greatest asset of the world. It is the beacon light guiding the destinies of millions of people. It is the source of illumination and inspiration. It is the bulwark and signpost of great significance.

To reach this dizzy height of God-realization is not an impossible achievement as supposed by men. It is within the compass of every human soul but it requires sacrifices of a unique order. It requires renunciation of the mind, the body and the senses. It means complete control of the triangular forces as represented by bodily desires, the cravings and grossness of the senses and flights and disorderliness of the mind.

God's universe is an open book to all. Its mysteries are covered with a veil, no doubt but that veil can be lifted up and man can see the invisible, with the eye of the hidden spirit within him. God's mysteries are never a sealed book to any one. But to see His hidden beauty, His glory, His power, the faculties hidden in man are to be opened and developed. The hidden eye must function. The deep longing and yearning for God must continually fan the inner flames and keep man alive to this fact that he has to give, not to take, that he has to give away his all in all for the furtherance of God's work in the universe. It is only when he reaches this state of perfection, the veil is lifted and he sees, that which was believed to be invisible, but which in actuality was never invisible, but always open. It is because man is so blind and prefers to grope in the dark than to see the sunlight, that things visible become invisible to him.

There is nothing hidden, nothing invisible in God's universe. It is all open to every one. But he must put on the glasses of the spirit to scan the universe which is made of spirit, not matter.

No man can live without God. He may in his ignorance exile God from his life. But sooner or later he must realize this fundamental fact that nothing exists in the universe except the will of God. God is the veiled substance on which hangs the whole tissue and fabric of His wide universe. He is the essence of everything. He is Law. His power is the highest in the universe. He is the moulder and builder of the destiny of every human soul. He is the architect of the whole spiritual edifice known as God's Kingdom. His power is boundless; His wisdom impenetrable; His goodness Infinite. His presence can be felt only in the heart, when it yearns and longs for Him from the very depths of its roots. He is unknown and unknowable to the millions, who scramble for things of the earth, earthy. But those devout souls, who give up everything in pursuit of God and His Eternal BLISS, eventually succeed in breaking open the bars that hide Him and feel His presence, as an infant sucking at the breast of its mother instinctively feels that she is her nourisher.

Man essentially being a spark of God, can not remain enamoured of earthly possessions for long. He must assert his spirit, which is innate and inmost in him and discard matter which is a bar to his real progress. Man's real progress is not in achievement of great distinction for earthly discoveries. The real progress is of only one type– the progress of the soul– the progress of the spirit – the progress of God in man– the progress of his divinity.

The vital spark of God in man when it is once ignited and enflamed can do wonders. It not only transforms the man's whole being but through him, God works His wonders for the transformation of the whole world.

No man ever lives alone. Even if he exiles himself and lives in wilderness, cut off from all human contacts, he becomes affiliated to God and when this alliance takes place, his inner vibrations reach millions of people and lift their souls from the morass of ignorance and darkness. He does good, invisible to the human eye but not invisible to God, whose ways are so mysterious and bountiful.

God wants all His erring children to come to Him.

He gives them spiritual fare when they hunger for Him. He shows them the light, when they grope in darkness and cry in anguish for a way out of their difficulties and doubts. There is no soul so sinful as not to be fit for redemption. Suffering is God's instrument – the unalterable decree of God – to bring the erring soul to its senses. It is God's plan that each soul shall evolve as it suffers and rise higher and higher in the scale of life. From darkness into light, from death into immortality–this is God's Eternal Law. His love is dynamic; His justice ever tempered with mercy; His kindness visible in every action.

To love God from the very depths of the heart is to win BLISS Eternal, Life Eternal, Wisdom Infinite. To love God is to win God's love and to win God's love is to capture all that is worth living for and dying for. It is the *summum bonum* of life. The longing for God is like inflaming the most vital portion in man for achievement of the highest in the universe.

Nothing can be achieved by man without a deep longing for God. This deep longing for God is the main key in opening the secret locks of God's universe. Whether a man is a *karma yogi or gnani* or a religionist, if he worships God from the very depths of his heart, with an unfailing and deep longing for God, he puts himself unmistakenly on the right way to God-realization. No man can ever long for God unless his soul is purified, his mind made a passive instrument of God and his desire and cravings are completely controlled.

It may appear what the above preaching has to do with *Romance of a Soul*, which is the title of this book. It has everything to do for the narrative which we are going to relate is that of a soul of no ordinary type. It is the narrative of a soul's longing for God. But for this longing the soul would have lost its romantic colourfulness. We associate the word "romance" with something unusually colourful and picturesque in man's life.

Love is the basis of romance. Feats of adventure, deeds of valour, also constitute romance. We speak of romantic literature, romantic dances, romantic music, romantic paintings, romantic art and romantic ways of living. But we rarely speak of soul's romance for, ordinarily, spirit plays no dominant part in man's activities. Man is carried away more by mundane attractions than by the idealism of the spirit. Few are stirred to the roots of their spirit. Only few are devoured by the flames of intoxicating love for divinity. Only few care to indulge in such a rare feast of the soul *viz.*, the longing and yearning for God and perfection of oneself after the pattern of God Himself.

We want more of soul's romance than romance of any other kind. Soul's romance means man's struggle in life for the ascendency of the spirit within him, for the triumph of virtue over evil, for the defeat and vanquishment of all that is Godless, soul-less and heartless. In the struggle of life, the head wins, the heart loses. In the scramble for loaves and fishes of life, one who has brain wins the race. The world's standards are so different from God's. Here and there we see a saint, a seer, a prophet of humanity, raising his head and hand and stopping the stream of man's rush for power and gain and directing it to a newer channel to peace and love and harmony. If a man rises from poverty to become a millionaire, the world applauds him and calls it a romantic career. If a man reaches the height of fame in arts, literature, politics, commerce, industry or in any other walk of life, he is worshipped as a hero and his romantic career is hailed with shouts of cheer.

This false standard of life has to change. There is only one kind of romance worthy of man's emulation and that is the romance of the soul. Each one should dream of romance, but romance of what? – the romance of the soul and not disgraceful romances of ballet dancers and society fops. They make life a gilded tapestry interwoven with sickening colours of dross and man's guilt. They call love suicides a romance. This is trash.

It is only when the heart is purified with love for God, we shall not hear of such sordid romances of love-sickness, love-hydrophobia. Love should not be prostituted into lust. This is what happens in the so called romantic books with which libraries of the world are to-day stocked. It not only means ruination of morals but a steady growth of poison in the human system which no drugs or the latest discoveries of science will avert.

God wants that the word 'romance' should be deleted from man's vocabulary except when it is used in connection with the soul's sublime efforts for its mastery in life. We want soul's romance and no other romance. The soul's triumph in its fight against the forces of evil is itself a romance. It is real, true romance – romance that should stir up man's heart and spirit and bring him nearer to God. The life of Socrates should be deemed romantic in the highest sense of the word. His was not a love romance in the sense understood by the world. Love for philosophy and love for all mankind constituted the basis of Socrates's romance. His love for Truth was so great that he disdained things of the earth, earthy and when he was accused and sentenced to death on a false charge of corrupting the morals of the Athenian youths, he willingly drank the cup of hemlock and died a martyr's death. In the history of the world there is no figure so colourful in its romantic career as Socrates, barring Christ and other prophets.

Christ, of all persons on earth, should be considered a person of the highest romantic charm. His life is an expression of the highest spiritual force extant in man. It is a life tinged with romance of the highest spiritual order. There was a romantic urge in Christ that made him an immortal figure. Among the immortals of the world from the most ancient time till the present day, there is none that we know of, that could be compared to Christ or Socrates in the romantic charm of their lives, lived in utter disregard of self and for the good of others in an ever increasing measure, out of great and ceaseless yearning and longing for God. Christ's life reads like a fairy tale; it is so full of spiritual romance. In the history of mankind from the dawn of civilization in the past there is only an attempt at demonstrating, that puny as man is, he is a master of the world in its physical aspects; not a word has so far been breathed out to any one of Christ's romantic career. All speak of him as Son of God. None recollects him as a most romantic figure, though the life of austerity and integrity that he led till he was crucified in his innocence gives a most exalted picture. Christ's crucifixion is a romance of the soul of the highest order.

Not only Socrates and Christ but the lives of other prophets, saints and seers, should be considered as romances of the highest order. We don't find romance of the soul only in celebrities. There is romance of the soul even in the common herdsman, the unskilled craftsman, the unaltered and undeterred peasant, the fisherman, the boatman, the labourer in the dock, the soldier who defends your country and the sailor who goes to the sea. Life is a battle, a struggle and in that playground of opposing forces of good and evil, he who takes the side of virtue and fights the evil, spreading joy and sunshine, plays the role of life not only correctly but his fight gives a colour to his life and that is real romance, – the romance of the soul.

When a man dedicates his life, whole-heartedly and entirely for the good of others and takes up some great cause such as advocacy of peace, campaigns against diseases such as tuberculosis, leprosy, cancer, plague, malaria etc., forming societies and associations for saving people from the scourge of sexual delinquency, aiding hospitals, infirmaries, creches, schools and industrial homes, founding churches and centres of learning, opening libraries, reading rooms and culture groups – he is really not only contributing towards man's uplift and accelerating his own spiritual growth, but is filling his life with a charm that is romantic and inspiring. To lead colour to an otherwise dull and drab canvas of life by an artistic mixture of soul's spirituality is real romance. To give a kiss for a kick is romance. To speak well of others who dispraise you, malign you, ridicule you and even abuse you and harm you in every way is romance. To give away even your last penny or to mortgage your very coat to help some one is romance. To befriend your enemy in distress is romance. To take things philosophically when the wind is against you and you bear patiently losses from every side, is romance.

A man who shows the qualities of fortitude, courage, mercy, friendliness, patience, charity, brotherliness and humility adds a romantic charm to his soul. He who empties his purse and pocket of the silvery bullets to fight against disease and poverty among people has a romantic soul. He who abandons his homeland and goes out in the wilderness to minister to the needs of the people of undeveloped and less-developed countries of the world is a hero, worthy of praise. His life is a romance of a high order. Doctors, missionaries, schoolmasters and pastors and all those who work in the slums -- they form a group of most romantic souls.

The above picture is enough to understand what is meant by romance of the soul, which is the only romance, man must concentrate his mind upon and none else. It is the only romance that has God's sanctity and sanction, all else is trash, putrid poison and disease.

The greatest romance of the soul is when man in his love and devotion for God, renounces everything and becomes a submissive tool in the hands of his Creator, who makes use of him, for spreading the mission of truth, goodwill, love and peace all throughout the world. Orators, musicians, poets and philosophers have a special role to play in life. Their very vocation demands a high standard of the soul – a soul saturated in God's beauty and glory. To express their inner beauty in a charming manner is an art which can be developed to perfection when the God-given talents are used for man's spiritual awakening and renaissance.

Soul is eternal, body is temporary. When such is the case, it is a short-sighted policy on the part of man to think of the body at the expense of the soul. When body decays, it is soul alone that survives. There is no such thing as death of the soul. Soul is the most important part of man, not the body. The body is a mere trapping, a cover, a sheath, a shell of no value except in its relationship with the indwelling soul. The body functions because of the indwelling soul. It ceases to function the minute the indweller leaves its temporary abode.

If the body is pampered, the soul starves. If the body is neglected, it ceases to function and the soul takes its flight. Both the courses are harmful. The first one leads to ruination of the soul. The second is called suicide. Anything that harms the soul is a sin. Anything that brings a precipitous ending to life by utter neglect of the body is also a sin. There is no romance in adultery, stealing, pick-pocketing, stock exchange manipulations, pompous display of wealth and riches, intriguing polities, garrulous talk and insipid writings. Those who commit suicide in frustration of their aims for personal aggrandisement are to be pitied. Suicide, unless it is committed from an altruistic motive or from a higher inner urge, is a sin, as bad as murder. There is no romance in a person committing suicide when thwarted in love affair. There is no romance, if out of false notion of self-exaltation, a man fasts unto death, either to terrorise others or to victimise them to his way of thinking. It is also a sin if a *sanyasin* refuses to take care of his body and exposes himself to death.

There is no spirituality in exposing one's body beyond the limits of human endurance. When we speak of crushing the body to awaken the soul within, it is used more in an allegorical sense *viz.*, that the body does not deserve our attention as the soul within. But that does not mean that the body should be starved to death. Lord Buddha tried that method and he failed in gaining *nirvana*. He eventually preached the middle course and it is really the most commendable.

Eat little, talk little, sleep little, – that is romance. Work ceaselessly, have an unlimited appetite for doing good to others without expectation of a return or reward – that is romance. Every thought, every word, every deed – they should be the outcome of a pure heart and in that measure only they sustain the soul.

The soul's romantic career starts from the cradle but it does not end with the grave. It carries its romance from birth to birth, from one incarnation to another incarnation, till perfected in every way, it ceases to inhabit the human body and makes its eternal home in the Spirit World. Such is the romance of the soul – a romance before which all other romances pale into insignificance.

Aspire to be romantic. We want poetry in life but not the hackneyed poetry of the pedlar who sells his merchandise from door to door, but real poetry that surges from the heart, the glow of which kindles the mind and the soul and brings joy all around.

Little things well done are better than great projects ill done. There is more beauty and grace in a tiny flower growing in a quiet corner than all the wealth of colour in a noisy market place.

There is greater romance in feeding the hungry and the naked with one's own hand than in donating large sums of money for gaining popularity. A pound of silent service is better than a ton of tall talk. Love for publicity is a mockery of the spirit. It is gruesome; it is uncouth; it is unromantic. Service rendered silently, however small it be, adds to the lustre of the soul. It is true romance. Men are in different phases of evolution. Just as in a triangle, the base occupies the greatest space and as we go towards the apex, it ends in a point, the space between the base and the apex becomes narrower and narrower, there are innumerable souls in the rudimentary state of evolution. Their number is the largest. As the soul goes on evolving, the number of evolved souls according to their state of evolution, becomes smaller and smaller, as we ascend from the base to the apex. The apex of the triangle represents the perfected soul–the Master in human body.

It takes countless incarnations to reach the state of perfection *i.e.*, adeptship. It is however in the hands of man to reduce the number of evolutions to reach the state of perfection. It is possible, but very few do it for they find the attempt beyond their capacity. However difficult it be, God has so arranged that after every birth and evolution, the soul advances in stature, however negligible it be in some cases. This is called the Law of Progression or Evolution. It is the destined lot of every one to reach the apex, starting from the base of the triangle. As he comes nearer and nearer to the apex, God gives him a guide, a Master to accelerate the speed of his evolution and bring him to the destined goal in as less time as possible. It is because of God's grace, when man stumbles or falls, He raises him up and clears the way for him. Without God's grace, no human soul can achieve its emancipation. God's grace is an indispensable item in man's ultimate progress to the goal.

No book of fiction can be so strange as the romance of the soul. Climbing upward and upward, as it evolves step by step and ultimately reaches the dizzy height of perfection after the pattern of God's own divinity. The load of suffering that it carries as it marches from one stage to another is the mark of a soul's romance, as it strives to overcome difficulties and obstacles in one desperate attempt to free itself of all embarrassments and entanglements. Historically viewed, nothing is so romantic as the soul's flight from one plane of action to another till after gaining all sorts of experiences both sweet and bitter, it makes the best use of them for its own perfection.

The soul's aura is an indicator of its progress. The colours change from time to time, as the soul evolves. When the lower colours change for yellow and blue, it is an indication of the soul reaching its emancipation. When the aura turns into a sheath of perfect whiteness, very rarely seen in a human soul, it is the indication of the soul's ascension to the highest height of perfection. Man becomes God in man, endowed with powers of far-reaching importance. The soul's romance reaches its climax when man is transformed into Godhood with infinite powers to do good to all mankind.

1

FIRST HUMAN BIRTH

AS A CHRISTIAN MONK

In the year of grace 1213, there was born in the house of a baron, a feudal lord, a child, whom its parents christened by the name of Petrico.

The child grew up into a very shy and reserved boy. He was quite unlike other children, especially his brothers, who loved sport and manly games of shooting and hunting. Petricio loved silence and solitude from the very commencement of his life. When the brothers laughed and giggled and played jokes, this boy would hardly take any interest in their hilarity and preferred to remain silent. He was teased and very often even practical jokes were played upon him. The poor boy bore it all quietly. His only solace was communion with God and Nature. From the very childhood, he felt that he was hearing some strange voice which kept him bewildered and he loved the music of that voice. He often felt thrilled when a sort of ecstatic joy swept him in his hours of silence and seclusion.

The boy grew up with a yearning and longing for the Invisible. He made Nature the object of deep contemplation. He loved to roam about in the fields and to climb the mountains of his homeland. Though shy and reserved, he showed great dexterity and intelligence. He was loved by his schoolmaster who looked upon the lad as a prototype of excellent virtues, clever, intelligent, ever kind and living.

His father wanted him to enter into some profession, but the boy as he grew in years, did not show the least inclination to any line of avocation. The parents were much disappointed. One day, he left the parental roof, leaving a note behind that he had made the world as his home and God, his protector. He wandered about from place to place, sleeping on stones under the canopy of the blue vault of the sky. Wherever he went, he sang the songs composed by him and played on the flute he carried. He spoke to the people who gathered round him of God and God alone. They laughed at him at first, but as he continued unfailingly in his addresses, they saw and were deeply impressed by his enthusiasm and devotion to God. He began to collect friends. They followed him also from place to place. They formed a band of pilgrims, who made the object of their lives to talk of God and God alone and create a sort of religious awakening.

As years passed by, Petricio's fame as an itinerant preacher spread far and wide throughout Italy and even in other countries of Europe. He soon founded an Order of Friars and built a monastery. This building in spite of ravages of time still exists, though in a dilapidated condition. It is taken care of by the people with great reverence and love, for it enshrines the remains of a man, who gave his all in all for God and to whom God was everything.

Even this great and holy man inspite of his great longing for God and his cloistered life was not perfect, not perfect in the sense that he had some weaknesses – the weaknesses that arise when man worships God from one angle only – the angle which he considers as the only angle of Truth. Holy and religious as he was, he fell a victim to the notice that the church founded by him was the only way to reach God. He led a fierce and fiery crusade against all those people who differed from his religious views. Though he loved God with all the fire of his rich heart, he emptied the fire of his anger on all those whom he considered as heathens, who did not believe in Christ, as the only Saviour of man and who did not follow the articles of his faith.

When this good and holy man passed away in the year 1349, a spell of silence fell upon the whole countryside. He was deeply loved and revered by millions of people. He was canonised thirty years after his death as a great saint of Christianity.

Let us now analyse the character of this man whose short narrative we have given above in the light of our observations at the commencement. Will his life be considered as a romance of the soul? Our answer is definitely in the affirmative.

There was romance in the lad when he bore all the jokes and pranks of his brothers against him. There was romance in him, when he disdained to accept the conventions of the day. There was romance in him when he preferred to go without meals and sports but loved his solitude and meditated and prayed in a silent corner in the midst of Nature's refreshing beauty. There was romance in him when he escaped from his father's house to lead the life of an itinerary preacher, sleeping in the streets at night in cold and wintry weather, careless of fatigue and comfort. There was romance in him when he spoke of God in that thrilling, rapturous manner, which turned even those who came to scoff at him into his devoted followers. There was romance in him, when he could exercise such a great and gripping influence upon the people as to collect large sums of money which he used for building a church and a monastery and in founding a Holy Order of Friars. His whole life from the cradle to the grave may be considered as a romance. And yet this man, though canonised as a saint, had to take birth again.

He was holy in the eyes of the world but it was holiness not of the transparent hue. It was holiness stained by the sin of religious bigotry. It was holiness which thrived upon popular prejudices and was fanned by the fire of a parochial outlook. It was holiness which lacked in universality of spirit and goodwill to all. It was holiness of the archaic, mediaeval type, symbolic of the age in which he was born and lived.

The prelate when he died did come over to the Spirit World with joyous delight. He was received by God's angels and in view of his purity, his life of dedicated service and his devotion of God, he was ushered straight off into the highest region of the Spirit

World, admissible to human souls. Here he spent a long time, visiting all the planes one by one, till he gained the knowledge of the working of God and the hidden mysteries of the universe. His soul was fully trained and equipped with powers with a view to its attaining success in its next incarnation on the earth plane.

Spirits living in the Spiritual Plane can stay there for five hundred to one thousand years. Those who are not able to cross the border of the lower astral plane are sent back to the earth in the span to twenty or twenty - five years. Those who are not able to go beyond the boundary of the higher astral world – and inhabitants of this plane are numerous – are sent away in the course of fifty to hundred years, according to their state of evolution. The mental world is considered the heavenly world where comparatively few spirits arrive. They stay in the mental plane for a longer time, say a century or two. The souls that enter into the Spiritual Plane are of two categories: (1) those who are liberated and have earned the passport of eternity; (2) those who have to return to the earth plane once again to perfect their evolution for attainment of eternal bliss.

The Spiritual Plane is the home of the Masters. The Masters are Adepts, perfected human souls who have gained the right of Eternal Bliss by the perfection of their lives in their last incarnation on the earth plane. Their work now is to guide humanity in the right channels of activity. These Masters have powers of extremely wide nature. They are links between men and God. They are humanity's greatest benefactors and helpers. But for the vigilance of the Masters who continually guide and control human souls, the world would be a wreckage – a mass of utter confusion and chaos. It is through the channel of their guidance, God is transforming humanity from its primitive state of barbarism and semi-savageness by slow stages of evolution and progression into a highly civilized and advanced state of civilization. This process of evolution will continue till every man reaches the state of perfection and becomes in turn a Master himself. It may take cycles of years to reach the millennium but such is God's plan and design, and what is planned and decreed by God must happen.

The prelate was most averse to take birth again. This was natural, for after tasting the waters of unalloyed bliss in the Spiritual Plane, no spirit would care to descend to the earth plane choked with human suffering and misery.

2

SECOND BIRTH AS A HINDU WOMAN

Who likes to eat a sour fruit after he has tasted sweet and juicy grapes? It is only a perfected soul that does it for to it sweetness and bitterness are the same. The prelate though saintly had not attained the liberation of his soul and God commanded that he should be reborn and complete his evolution on the earth plane. God gave him a chance to earn his emancipation by giving him a birth in a totally different environment and in a different faith. The prelate was reborn in a Hindu family in Southern India.

We shall not give the name of the child so born for it makes no difference what name it bore. The child was a female child, destined to play a unique role a moulding the lives and destinies of countless persons who came in contact with her. The child grew up into a maiden and blossomed into sweet womanhood. The beauty of her soul was rare. She married but her married life was a dismal affair. She married though totally averse to marriage, for the simple reason that the custom of her society left her no choice. She was in fact, sold in marriage by her parents. Hardly when she was out of teens, she was given away as a bride to a person more than double her age and for whom she had no liking, no reverence, no respect, no fondness. Her father's word was law and she had to bend down to his will. There was no joy in her heart when she married. She thought she was joined with a log of wood. It was to her not a marriage ceremony but ascending the funeral pyre. But her sense of duty was so great, that after she was forced in marriage to the man, she did not like, she greeted him as her lord and obeyed him and served him faithfully. She bore children and encountered difficulties and torments, few would undergo with such heroism of spirit and sacrifice as she did.

Unlettered and illtaught, she knew more of God and His divinity than all the learned *pundits* of her time. Her power of intuition was great and that was her guiding principle. Her heart was open to every cry of pain and anguish. She succoured the poor and was always by the bedside of the ailing. Her life was a continuous round of service for which she got no applause except mute gratitude of the hundreds and thousands whom she relieved of their pain and suffering. Dedicated to silent service, her name was a household word in the place where she lived. People knew her for her charity, her loyalty, her sense of duty, her sacrifice, her gentility, her endurance and above all her spirit of service without any distinction of class or creed. She had no scruples even to associate with persons of the lowest caste, though the custom of her Hindu society forbade such intercourse. To her all were same and she treated them not as outcastes but her fellow associates and members of her household. She did not at all mind the bitter words of fury that were hurled on her by her husband and the *brahmins* when she associated with them in such a familiar manner. The high *pundits* of her city would have declared her as an outcast but for her womanhood which was a defence against their onslaughts.

She led a life of long drawn-out agony but brave and noble as she was, she never uttered a word of complaint to any one. On the contrary, she gave herself up entirely to ministering to the wants and sufferings of others. Her heart overflowed with the milk of human kindness. There was love in her eyes. Her feet always carried her wherever there was a cry of pain and agony. She considered all forsaken children as her own. She mothered them and brought solace and cheer into countless homes. She was looked upon as an *avatar* of God in the slums she visited, by the denizens of the dark dens. She was a veritable goddess, so thoughtless and regardless of her own gain and so imbued with the pain and suffering of others.

This woman would have gained her emancipation but being a mother, her motherly instincts, she could not conquer. She was exceedingly indulgent to her children and spoiled them. Her extreme love and affection for her children made her overlook their faults. They were an antithesis to her own sublimity of character. They were a constant source of anxiety to her – an anxiety which was brought upon her by her own weakness in dealing with them. Her up-bringing of them was wrong.

It is a strange study of character, that a person utterly unselfish and of sacrificial ardour – a source of blessing of thousands, could also be a miserable failure in her own home in spite of her love, devotion and loyalty both to her husband and children.

God wants man to act in an unattached manner. Attachment is a sin. The woman's attachment to her children was the cause of her failure to secure emancipation of her soul, which in all other respects she had already gained. Detachment is a principal plank in renunciation; it is a principal pillar in the edifice of God-realization.

This good, noble, brave woman of dauntless courage and most mild and loving nature passed away in ripe years. There is no record of her greatness enshrined in any book. To the world, she was just an ordinary soul. Being a householder, she was never noticed as a woman of saintly character or reckoned as a woman of high spiritual eminence. Her virtues were forgotten as her body was put on the burning pyre and a great soul slipped away from the world, unmourned, unnoticed, unwept. Such is the wanton wickedness of the world which applauds only those who make a bravado of their strength and might but hardly notice the fact that in the hovels of the poor, in the dark dens of life, among the rustics and the so-called illiterate, there is more of God, than in the skilled orator or the cunning politician, who wins the applause of the world by the display of his faculties, meant to be used only for the uplift of the poor and the lowly in a quiet, silent manner.

When the woman passed away there was no obituary in any paper. But she left behind in countless hearts she had lifted, the memory and the fragrance of her angelic deeds and good nature.

The soul which had inhabited the body of the Catholic priest, also inhabited the body of a Hindu woman, when it took birth again on the earth plane after a long gap of several centuries and we have described the characteristics formed in each incarnation. To all intents and purposes the prelate was a more powerful man but that does not mean that the Hindu woman was less spiritual. On the contrary from the higher standard of the judgment of the Spirit world the Hindu woman's soul should be considered as having evolved and progressed further. Generally speaking, each incarnation marks the progress of a human soul Progress takes place at each turn of the soul's incarnation on the earth plane. Very rarely there is a set back. The reason why the soul progresses and never retards is that it makes use of the experiences of the past lives. When a man dies and leaves the world behind, his soul carries into itself the memory and fragrance of its past virtues and loses sight of its failings. These virtues are strengthened and more are added as the soul evolves in each successive incarnation.

Truly speaking, taking everything into consideration, the Hindu woman though much less known to the world than the Catholic prelate, was far more heroic and there was a greater romance of the soul in her than her counterpart, the prelate of the earlier incarnation. We thus see the ladder of progression, how the soul evolves from one birth to another, till perfected, its peregrinations to the earth plane in search of experiences are stopped.

3

THIRD BIRTH AS A PARSI

On the 4th October 1888, in the city of Poona in India, the same soul which in its past incarnations had gathered experiences as a Catholic priest and a Hindu woman, took birth in a Parsi family, following Zoroastrian faith. He was named Minocher K. Spencer. Upto the moment of this narration, there is no record of any upheaval associated with this soul's performances, an upheaval of world-wide nature.

This soul has gone through fiery ordeals from its birth, unknown to the world, but every event of which is recorded in God's book, in letters of gold, This soul has reached the uppermost rung in the ladder of perfection. This soul which sought liberation in its earlier incarnations but failed has at last succeeded in gaining its object. It is to-day a liberated soul, but known to none in the world except God and the

Masters. To give a detailed account of this soul's doings would fill a volume. This work we shall leave to be done at a later stage in a different role. But it is necessary to stress on some of the most salient points in the career of this soul for the enlightenment of the world.

It is the general notion that God-realization can be attained only by putting on the yellow robe of a *sanyasin* and forsaking the world entirely.This is the Indian conception of renunciation. There is no boubt that the India *Yoga* system is the highest and the best in the world. But it has to be understood and studied in all its ramifications. This ancient teaching of Indian saints and seers requires introduction in all the countries of the world. But its interpretation should be modern. It should be adapted now to the fast changing circumstances of life and thoughts of man. A man can practise renunciation sitting in his own home surrounded with comforts of a home life, as well, if not better than a real *sanyasin* paractising *tapas* in a jungle or in a mountain cave, away from the giddy buzz of human tongues and voices.

Renunciation is the attitude of the mind. You must renounce the world by you mind, i.e., even if you be surrounded by the comforts of a home life, partake of them, but with absolutely a detached mind. Perfect detachment of the mind is a *sine-qua-non* in renunciation.

The question that arises is whether it is possible for a *maharajah,* a statesman, a politician, an industrialist, a lawyer, an engineer, a doctor, a merchant, a shipbuilder and so forth, to be in the world and at the same time, have no cravings for riches, name, fame, glory, power etc. To be in the thick of worldly life and at the same time to practise rigid austerity and lead a life of absolute desirelessness, keeping the mind centred on God and God alone and having no other thought than of doing good to all mankind without expectation of any return or reward–

this is renunciation.

People must change their ideas about renunciation. Just as people have forgotten the fundamentals of religion and have religionised religion to suit their way of thinking by adumbration of rites and rituals of meaningless nature the true conception of renunciation in lost and a false sense is propagated. In India, today there are millions of so called *fakirs* and *sadhus*, who put on saffron robes and rugged garments and lead a lazy life, depending upon the doles which they collect from door to door for their existence. The class of religious mendicants must entirely go. There is no soul romance at all in begging for food and roaming about listlessly and aimlessly from place to place without doing anything. God does not want parasites to flourish in religious garbs. God does not want rituals and dogmas to be mixed up with fundamental teachings of the prophets.

The teachings of religion are for the masses.

Renunciation is meant only for those few souls who are hungary for God and whose longing to unveil the secrets of the universe is so great. This renunciation can be practised in two ways, either by leaving one's home and leading an excluded life in solitude and in perfect silence or by living in the world of multiple activities but keeping the mind perfectly cool and calm in all vicissitudes of life, without being disturbed in the least by the displeasure of the world and without seeking any praise or becoming elated by success. Perfect equanimity of the mind in all weathers is the test of one's renunciation. This quietude of the mind will be attained by leading a life of simplicity, austerity, purity, altruism, self-lessness, sacrifice, friendliness with all, tolerance, endurance, fortitude and humility.

Desirelessness and detachment form the main pillars of renunciation, whether you practise that renunciation on the top of a mountain or in the thick of your busy, giddily world. The choice is yours. It all depends upon your own temperament, your own idiosyncrasies, your power of endurance and your environment. Whatever you do, remember the fundamentals of religion and renunciation. God-realization is within the compass of a man, whether he be a *fakir* or king. It may appear very strange how a king in a palace, surrounded with all the pomp and power of worldly order can attain to God-realization. But in reality it is not strange at all, if the king surrounded with all the paraphernalia associated with his royalty, can at the same time be detached. Detachment of the mind in such circumstances is more difficult of attainment. But it is not impossible.

The idea of opening monasteries and *ashrams* by saints and sages where aspirants for God-realization be accepted is a good one and it should be encouraged.

To practise detachment of the mind while leading a worldly life is out of question. But though difficult, it is possible to attain detachment of the mind by living in the world but away from worldly foibles and gaities and worldly ways of doing things. If you can maintain your isolation and independence even when you are in the thick of worldly associations, you will be able to gain mastery over your mind and will not allow it to be attracted by external phenomena and daily occurrences.

In order to strengthen your mind with the sense of detachment two things are absolutely necessary viz. (1) great longing for God and (2) prayers and meditation for long hours. A man may be a *karma yogi* and a *gnani* but without longing for God and prayers and meditation it is impossible for him to attain the goal of God-realization. In fact, the desire to work for others, without expectation of any return or reward comes only when there is a great yearning and longing for God, which is accelerated by means of silence, prayers, seclusion and deep meditation. Whether one is a *karma yogi* or *gnani*, a life of silence, solitude, prayers and deep meditation must take preedence over the other activities. He must set a part a certain portion of his time, while discharging his duties, for prayers and miditation.

A study of the lives of prophets, saints and seers should convince any one that solitude and silence, prayer and meditation are vital parts in man's life-career for the attainment of the goal of God-realization. They are indispensable and man should not arrogate that a life of mere altruistic activity is enough.

This great longing for God which is the first and most important step towards the goal of God-realization comes to a man at times in the early years of his life and at times later on. As soon as this inner urge arises, the feeling of indifference towards everything grips him. It is a preparation to get out from the clutches of *maya* and slowly and steadily he leaves off all the worldly ways of living and learns the art of detachment.

This is exactly what happened in the case of the

soul that we have just described. Born in a Parsi home, the boy grew up in the traditions of the home and his race. Shy and backward, he still had no idea or conception of the future. He dreamt like every young boy and man and scrambled through life's clumsy ways as best as he could, bearing kicks and learning grim lessons of life without exultation of the soul. But he did not know that the kicks he got, the ordeals he passed through, the misfortunes he met were all meant to cultivate in the soul a feeling of revolt against the godlessness of the world at large. Honest to the core, with the highest sense of duty which he had inherited from his past incarnations, he cast his lot in favour of Ahura Mazda, his Lord and God and pursued manfully his way in life, holding high the banner of Truth which he loved the most. Had he wished, he could have amassed wealth, married a society woman, reared children and gained name and fame. He was however saved from the world's *maya*, because of his experiences in the past incarnations. The majority suffer because of their past *karma.* He had very little of *karma* to wipe off and when this was done, he was taken charge of by a Master immediately, under God's orders.

The last five or six years of this man's life make a most romantic history. It is a real, thrilling romance of the soul. He was gripped with a secret longing for God. All the latent virtues which he had inherited from his past births blossomed out into full growth. He left business. He gave away all he had. He cut himself away from all the giddy ways of the world. He took to a life of solitude, prayers and meditation, making his home, God's alter, his heart, God's temple.

It was felt in the beginning that the soul would again fail in winning its liberation but it was not so. The Science of Spiritualism opened the door for the soul's awakening. It created a strange revolution in the whole make up of the man. He took to it like fish takes to water. He blundered, he suffered, he was ridiculed, he was attacked but he never wavered for a moment. Fascinated by this strange science, he rushed headlong into its vortices. He was remoulded. He developed the psychic powers of both auto-writing and clairaudience. He was thrilled. He wrote a book called, *The Other World* which created a sensation. His love to probe into the mysteries of the universe increased with every step he took. This fascinating science made him a new man. Had his motive been a mere curiosity or an avidity to play with spirits, he would have been entirely lost. It was his purity of mind and extreme longing and love for God that saved him from ruination which would have become inevitable if he had not succeeded in avoiding contact with low spirits. On the contrary, it brought him into contact with Masters and Spirits of the Higher Regions. God ordered Spirit Master Rishi Ram Ram to take the soul under his special protection.

A new method was devised whereby he could contact and hear spirits without physical frustration and mental disorder. It was a gift specially conferred upon him in order to enable him to contact the Masters and to be in thick with the Invisible World, without the least fear of frustration of any kind.

It was Ram Ram who made him pay visits to two God-relized souls on the earth plane, *viz.*, Meher Baba and Sri Ramana. The former only ignited his soul to make an assault on the fortress of the invisible World with still greater fury and force. But the latter quickened his soul for *nirvana,* which he gained after his visit to the Seer's *ashram* in Arunachala. His visit to Ramana, the Sage of Arunachala, was a red letter day in the annals of the life of the aspirant. It worked a revolution in his heart, mind and soul. He gave up everything entirely. He gave up even his leper work in which he was totally absorbed.

It was all planned by God. He took to solitude and deep contemplation and meditation. Continuous contact with his Master Ram Ram and the study of the Scriptures, which enabled him to write a series of books on Spiritual Philosophy and Religion published by the Spiritual Healing Centre of Combatore, – an institution founded under the guidance of the same Master, Ram Ram – developed his soul to such an extent that Ram Ram was ordered by Sai Baba as *Ahura Mazda* (God) to relax his training and to hand over the aspirant for further training and guidance to God Himself.

Such a boon is rarely conferred upon a human soul. But there were weighty reasons for such consideration shown to him. The aspirant by the dint of his continuous efforts to realize God succeeded in winning God's love. He chose him therefore to become His messenger on earth to spread the message of Love and Peace and Goodwill and to pave the way for the unification of all mankind into one holy bond of Universal Brother-hood.

Such is the simple story of this soul which is

speeding fast towards the fulfilment of God s order to be His messenger on the earth before it is called away to the Other World–its home eternal.

The aspirant has been fully trained and equipped for his mission. God has issued orders to the masters to befriend and help him, for, the opposition against him would be strong and most unruly when the poor man commences his mission as ordered by God. This opposition would die away in no time for it is God's law that Truth must triumph and the aspirant is an emissary of Truth, specially ordained to spread the message of Truth to clear the dark dens of ignorance and apostasy and bring in God's ray of light and illumination. Ram Ram, Christ, Zoroaster, Buddha and Lord krishna are the guiding angels whom God has appointed to help the youthful soul in this performance of God's mission. These Masters are his guides and friends. It is to stop another world war breaking out, to establish peace on earth and to introduce religio-socio-politic and economical revolutionary changes which are so greatly needed that God is sending this emissary of Love and Goodwill for the welfare and uplift of the people of the world, torn and worn out, depressed and depraved by the vicious circle in which the world is moving so relentlessly and callously.

This man having won his liberation could have been called away to live eternally in the Spirit World. In spite of failing health, he has accepted God's invitation to work for the remaining span of his extended life. It is a most laborious piece of work but however strenuous it be, with the powers given unto him by God and under God's own direction and guidance, coupled with the constant co-operation of the Masters, it will prove a labour of love and joy. Welcome in all respects. The object of this tract is to prepare the world for great. Changes that are eminent (1954).

4

EPILOGUE

In this life, Monocher K. Spencer was able to fulfil the greatest ambition of his soul to realize God - see God face to face, as a result of the great love of and intense spiritual training under his Spirit Master Rishi Ram Ram and God Almighty in the form of Fakir Sai Baba. He has left behind a thrilling account of his spiritual pursuit as such in his remarkable memoirs *How I Found God* — a 1396-page book which has been condensed and edited by Dr. S.P. Ruhela. He did see God face to face in early 1958 and soon therefore he left this world at the age of 70, to join the Spirits of the Sprititual Plane.

NEW ERA

A New Era is opening out for mankind, a New Era of world Religion, a New Era of world Polity, a New Era of Knowledge and Wisdom. The New Religion will be broad based like the great pyramids on Universal Love. World Polity will be broad based on Equality, Brother-hood, co-operation and service which will support the great future edifice at the basic foundation.

Humanity is entering upon a New Era of constructive co-operation. Individuals have to keep the Goal before them and co-operate with one another and with society as a whole. The world of humanity will become one family of nations when peace and amity will reign over them inspite of different colours and creeds. The message for the New Era is "Love All - Love God and seek out more ways of loving Man and God."

–Message of the Spirit Master Rishi Ram Ram

PRAYER

"O God, we pray that we may be soon launched into a New Era of one World Religion, one World Polity, one World Civilisation, one World Humanity based on the foundations of equality and brotherhood, service and co-operation.

We pray that our scientists may now begin to study the inner worlds and give us the benefit of their researches. It is not only the union of all mankind that we seek, but the union of the whole universe, the discarnate co-operating with the incarnate spirits for the glory of The Kingdom. It is by means of universal love and prayers, that we shall build up a new kingdom of the spirit".

(Late) Yogi M.K. Spencer
Author of HOW I FOUND GOD

PRAYER FOR WORLD PEACE

Adorable Presence!
Thou Who art within and without, above and below and all around, Thou Who art interpenetrating the very cells of our beings, Thou Who art the Eye of our eyes, the Ear of our ears, the Heart of our hearts, the Mind of our minds, the Breath of our breaths, the Life of our lives and the Soul of our souls, Bless us, Dear God, to be aware of Thy Presence, now and here. This is all that we ask of thee.

May all of us be aware of Thy Presence in the East and the West, in the North and the South. May Peace and Goodwill abide among individuals as well as communities and nations! This is our earnest Prayer.

May Peace be unto all.

(Late) Swami Omkar

SOME SELECT PRESS OPINIONS ON *ROMANCE OF A SOUL*

"The book gives glimpses of the three lives of a soul, the first as a Catholic Priest of the thirteenth century, the second as a Hindu Lady of South India, a great worker for the poor and destitute, and the last as a Parsi gentleman born in October 1888. The doctrine of rebirth shows that progress is achieved from life to life provided the soul has strong affinities to God realisation ...... This is an interesting account ..."

— *The Hindu, Madras*

"The story book is written for the welfare and uplift of the people of the world and to draw them from a life of depravity and strife to one of Godliness, Love and Peace."

— *The Hindustan Times, New Delhi*

"The book carries much simple and impressive wisdom and should be welcome to every one who is making his way towards the light."

— The Forum, London

"The very interesting book giving an account of the three births of a soul. Lofty and admirable."

— The Hyderabad Gazette

"The Spiritual careering or way-faring through different lives of a blessed soul is given in this book. Real Romance is soul's triumph over evil and realisation of God"

— The Astrological Magazine, Bangalore

"This is a useful booklet giving a lucid explanation about the *Atma* and physical body. Philosophical explanation about how the development and evolution of the *Atma* can be achieved has been given in simple language."

— The Koiser-i-Hind

"The book contains many home truths and beautiful passages and has provocative value all its own"

Life, Coimbatore.